BOSTON'S FREEDOM TRAIL

Trace the Path of American History

EIGHTH EDITION

Illustrations by
JACK FROST

Text by
ROBERT BOOTH

Revised by
CINDI D. PIETRZYK

travel

Guilford, Connecticut

The prices and rates listed in this guidebook were confirmed at press time. We recommend, however, that you call establishments to obtain current information before traveling.

Text design by Gina Grasso
Map by Rusty Nelson © Morris Book Publishing, LLC

ISSN 1559-1808
ISBN 978-0-7627-4769-6

Printed in the United States of America
10 9 8 7 6 5 4 3 2

CONTENTS

FOREWORD

For 175 years the Freedom Trail in Boston was a concept without a name. In 1950 a Boston newspaperman, William G. Schofield, came to the realization that the greatest number of sites sacred to the beginnings of our Republic anywhere in the United States were located in Boston, and moreover they were all within easy walking distance of one another. Then, in a moment of inspiration, he conceived the name Freedom Trail.

Previously each site had its own organization and its individual idea of how to present itself to the public; as a result, the planning of an orderly visit was at best confusing, and the less-than-studious visitor might easily go away having missed something significant. Now, as the Freedom Trail has brought all of these places together under the aegis of the Freedom Trail Foundation, it is easy for the visitor to get a rounded and balanced view of the historic sites and through such an experience to enhance his or her knowledge of American history. Most important, under the confederation that now exists, there is no compromise in the individuality with which each site is presented.

This has been worked out over a period of time, thanks to the efforts of many groups, including the Advertising Club of Boston, the Greater Boston Convention and Visitors Bureau, the Freedom Trail Commission, and, most recently, the National Park Service, which today plays a vital part in the maintenance and interpretation of the sites along the Trail. This book is thus intended to present to the reader a package in which you will find admirably described many of

Boston's significant historic places. We of the Freedom Trail Foundation welcome you to our city and trust that this booklet will help you make your visit both a memorable and an enjoyable experience.

>—*Charles F. Adams, former chairman of the
>Freedom Trail Foundation*

Boston's Freedom Trail

FREEDOM TRAIL SITES AND OTHER HISTORIC STRUCTURES

The numbers on this page correspond with the numbers on the map on pages vi and vii.

1. Boston Common
2. State House
3. The Beacon
4. Park Street Church
5. Granary Burying Ground
6. King's Chapel and Burying Ground
7. Benjamin Franklin's Statue
8. The Old Corner Bookstore
9. Site of Franklin's Print Shop
10. Old South Meeting House
11. Site of Benjamin Franklin's Birthplace
12. Old State House
13. Site of the Boston Massacre
14. Faneuil Hall
15. Quincy Market
16. Boston Tea Party Ships and Museum
17. Paul Revere's House
18. Saint Stephen's Church
19. Paul Revere Mall
20. Old North Church
21. Copp's Hill
22. USS *Constitution*
23. Bunker Hill

Ⓣ indicates entrance/exit for rapid transit stations. The name of the station appears next to the Ⓣ. The dotted line indicates the Freedom Trail walking tour.

VISITOR INFORMATION

The Freedom Trail is one of the most popular walking tours in America. It covers approximately 3 miles and is easy to follow. The path is well marked by painted red lines or red bricks set into the pavement. Each site is identified by a distinctive marker or sign. Bear in mind that the Freedom Trail is a walking tour. Much of the Trail meanders through the twisting and curved streets that are the original paths and byways established by the first colonists. Do not attempt to drive the Trail. The best way to see everything is to walk.

The Freedom Trail Foundation offers a variety of tours for those who don't wish to go it alone. Check out their Web site, www.thefreedomtrail.org, for more information.

If you do decide to go it alone, I highly recommend the Freedom Trail Foundation's audio file that you can either download as an MP3 file onto your player or iPod, or listen to by picking up an audio player at the Visitor Information Center on the Common. Either way, you pay a $15 fee, but it's worth it. Have the kids listen to it on the way to Boston so they can be ready for what they're about to see or enjoy it yourself before, during, and after your tour! There are several drop-off points for these players along the Trail. This audio file has character voices and allows you to feel like you are back in colonial Boston as you walk through history. There's even a scavenger hunt for the children.

The National Park Service also offers tours along the trail. These begin every half hour from the park visitor center opposite the Old State House on the Common. There is a charge.

If you prefer to ride, there are trolley tours, but these are unofficial and may not take the rider to many of the sites along the Trail. Many parts of the Trail are not accessible by car, bus, or any means of wheeled transportation except bicycle. This book includes the official sites, as well as other important structures along the Trail that require excursions off the red trail.

You may pick up the trail anywhere along the route, but the most convenient and logical starting points are Boston Common or the USS *Constitution* in Charlestown.

Many of the sites along the Trail are free and allow you to stop, visit, and explore, while others charge admission. The three museums along the Trail, the Old South Meeting House, Old State House, and Paul Revere's House, now offer a discounted admission rate of $11 for adults and $3 for children ages six to eighteen. This one rate allows you entrance to all three museums. Tickets can be purchased online at www.paulreverehouse.org/trail but can also be purchased at either the Old South Meeting House or the Old State House. If your trip is in less than two weeks, it is recommended that you purchase the tickets once you hit town as opposed to online.

Boston is equipped with an efficient public transportation system. Buses operate along the route of the Freedom Trail about every ten to fifteen minutes, seven days a week, generally from 6:00 a.m. to midnight. The Massachusetts Bay Transportation Authority's (MBTA) Web site at www.mbta .com provides information about which station is nearest to each of the sites as well as schedules, routes, and fares. Information is also available by calling (800) 392-6100.

Bus fare ranges from $1.25 to $1.50 for adults; children eleven and younger ride free with an adult. Subway fare runs from $1.70 to $2.00 per person. Many stations and the information booth on Boston Common display free subway maps. Visitor passes, which cost $9 per person for one day and $15 per person for seven days, give you unlimited rides. In many stations there are vending machines where

WHAT HAPPENED WHEN
ON THE FREEDOM TRAIL

1630 The Puritans pitch their tents on Boston Common

1630 Sir Isaac Johnson is buried in his garden lot, soon to become King's Chapel Burying Ground

1656 Mary Dyer, Margaret Jones, and Mistress Anne Hibbins lose their lives for allegedly being witches

1660 Old Granary Burying Ground is laid out

1676 The Great Fire destroys many homes and buildings in Boston

1688 Sir Edmund Andros appropriates land for what will become King's Chapel

1710 King's Chapel congregation grows and the building is expanded

1711 Another huge blaze destroys a third of colonial Boston

1713 The Old State House is built

1721 James Franklin (Ben's brother and mentor) launches the *New-England Courant*

1723 Old North Church is erected

1729 The Old South Meeting House is built

1732 Benjamin Franklin begins *Poor Richard's Almanac*

1742 Peter Faneuil presents Boston with a market

1749 Governor William Shirley lays the cornerstone for the new King's Chapel

1753 The original King's Chapel is demolished to make way for the new one

1754 The new King's Chapel is completed

1765 The Stamp Act is levied by the British Parliament

1767 Parliament enacts the Townshend Revenue Bill, allowing it to tax imported goods to the colonies

1768 British troops invade and occupy Boston

1769 Royal Governor Francis Bernard flees to England

1770 The Boston Massacre occurs, the first blood shed in the American Revolution

1771 Thomas Hutchinson is appointed acting Royal Governor

1773 The Boston Tea Party takes place

1775 Paul Revere makes his famous midnight ride

1775 The Battle of Bunker Hill is fought

1776 The Declaration of Independence is publicly read to Bostonians for the first time

1795 Construction of the Massachusetts State House commences

1797 The USS *Constitution* is launched

1798 The Massachusetts State House is completed

1802 The cornerstone for Saint Stephen's Church is laid

1804 Saint Stephen's Church is completed and dedicated

1806 Charles Bulfinch rebuilds and expands Faneuil Hall after it is destroyed by fire

1807 The crest of Copp's Hill is removed for use as a millpond landfill

1811 Beacon Hill's crest is removed for landfill

1812 American Congress declares war on Britain

1817 The gallows on the Common are taken down

1822 Boston officially becomes a city

1823 Josiah Quincy is elected mayor of Boston

1824 General Lafayette visits Boston

1825 The old Town Dock area is filled in to meet demands for more market space

1825 Quincy Market is built

1825 The cornerstone for the monument at Bunker Hill is laid

1820s Municipal concerts begin to be held on the Common

1829 William Lloyd Garrison gives his first public antislavery address at Park Street Church

1830 Animals are banished from grazing on the Common

1834 Another 45 feet are added to the monument at Bunker Hill as construction continues

1840 Sarah Josepha Hale holds her fair to raise money to finish the monument at Bunker Hill, laying the groundwork for future women's organizations

1843 The Bunker Hill monument is finally completed and dedicated, the first monument built through public donation

1845 Cotton Hill is leveled and used to fill a millpond at its foot

1849 Charles Sumner delivers his "The War System of Nations" speech to the American Peace Society at Park Street Church

1856 The statue in honor of Benjamin Franklin is erected

1863 John Hancock's house is torn down

1965 Martin Luther King Jr. addresses thousands on the Common

1979 Pope John Paul II celebrates Mass for the public on the Common

2005 Cindy Sheehan addresses antiwar protesters

you put money on your CharlieCard to receive reduced fares. It's easy, and there's usually someone there to give you a hand in figuring out what you need and where you want to go.

Wheelchair travelers and persons sixty-five years of age or older may obtain reduced-fare passes from the MBTA's Office for Transportation Access at Back Bay Station or at the new Senior/T.A.P. ID Replacement Office located at Downtown Crossing Station on the Summer Street Subway Concourse between Washington and Chauncy Streets, weekdays, 8:30 a.m. to 5:00 p.m. For more information call (617) 222-5976 or (617) 222-5854 (TTY). The MBTA strives to have all their buses and stations wheelchair acces-

sible. For more information visit www.mbta.com/riding_
the_t/accessible_services/ or call (617) 222-3200 or (617)
222-5146 (TTY).

That's what you need to know. For further information
contact the Greater Boston Convention and Visitors Bureau
at (888) SEE-BOSTON or www.bostonusa.com. You may
also wish to visit the following Web sites:

- www.cityofboston.gov
- www.cityofboston.gov/freedomtrail/
- www.thefreedomtrail.org
- www.celebrateboston.com (gives closest MBTA stops
  as well as other information about the sites)
- www.iboston.org/pap/freedom.htm offers a cool inter-
  active Freedom Trail map

Good luck and happy history hunting!

BOSTON COMMON

Bounded by Park, Tremont, Boylston, Charles, and Beacon Streets

There's nothing common about Boston Common, America's oldest public park. Set on more than forty-four acres south of the Charles River and west of Boston Harbor, the Common is the starting point for the Freedom Trail.

The Common itself has seen more than 377 years of history. John Winthrop, the first governor of Massachusetts, and his Puritan followers first pitched their tents here in 1630. As the settlement grew, land was set aside for such important public uses as pasturage for goats and cows and for public punishment and executions.

The Puritans' preference for humiliation and ridicule as a means of enforcing their unyielding laws was evident in their public punishments. For thievery, those caught could be branded on the forehead with a letter *B* or whipped if caught twice. For a third offense the punishment was death by hanging in the public gallows on the Common. Other offenders were dunked in ponds, once numerous on the Common. Those ponds were nothing like Frog Pond, found on the Common today. No, not a children's wading pool, but a murky body of water filled with snakes, frogs, and other slimy water-dwelling critters. Definitely not a pleasant experience.

Some of the unfortunate citizens who met their punishment on the Common included William Robinson and Marmaduke Stevenson, who were convicted of being Quakers and were launched into eternity by hanging. Mary Dyer, Margaret Jones, and Mistress Anne Hibbins, proven consorts of His Satanic Majesty, were expunged from the Divine State. For unspecified crimes against the settlers, Matoonas, an Algonquian Indian sagamore, or subordinate chief, was tied to a tree and shot in 1656. These occasions were declared general holidays and attracted great crowds on the Common.

The land was also used as a military parade ground for the local "trayn-band," or militia. Before and during the early years of the Revolution, British regiments encamped on Boston Common.

It wasn't always violence on the Common, however. In 1824, when General Lafayette made his goodwill trip to the young democracy, Boston's schoolchildren turned out on the Common to sing "La Marseillaise." The general was also honored by 1,200 people at a public banquet under a canopy on the Common.

The Common continued to evolve and was used as pastureland until 1830, when the animals were banished. The gallows were taken down in 1817. In the late 1820s, the Society for the Suppression of Intemperance convinced Mayor Harrison Gray Otis that he could "promote order and suppress an inclination to riot and intemperance" by holding municipal concerts on the Common. Ever since, music lovers have gathered in the shade of towering oaks for band concerts and crowded under moonlit skies for performances by popular entertainers.

The twentieth century brought its own movers and shakers. The Reverend Martin Luther King Jr. addressed thousands on the Common in 1965, Pope John Paul II celebrated a public Mass here in 1979, Gloria Steinem advanced the feminist revolution on these grounds at the turn of the twenty-first century, and Cindy Sheehan addressed antiwar protesters in 2005.

With all its contemporary appeal, the Common continues to pay tribute to the past by providing a setting for many notable sculptures. The Soldiers and Sailors Monument, whose figures personify history and peace, rises like a vision

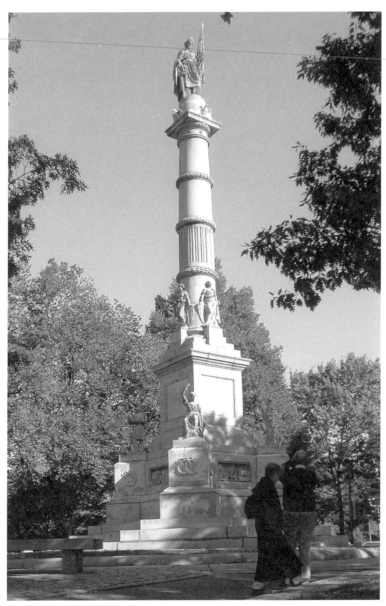

Soldiers and Sailors Monument on Boston Common memorializes all those who stood up for what they believed in. © 2005 CITY MAPS INC.

from a hilltop. Brewer Fountain stands tall just steps from the visitor's kiosk. Donated by Gardner Brewer in 1868, it depicts the mythical figures of Neptune, Galatea, Amphitrite, and Acis. The palette-shaped monument just within the fence of the Central Burying Ground at the corner of Tremont and Boylston Streets honors painter Gilbert Stuart, who is buried in one of the unmarked graves.

The most famous sculpture is undoubtedly the Robert Gould Shaw and Fifty-fourth Regiment Memorial by Augustus Saint-Gaudens at the corner of Park and Beacon Streets, facing the State House. This bronze memorial commemorates the bravery of the first black regiment to serve in the Civil War. Their colonel, the twenty-six-year-old Robert Gould Shaw, son of a prominent Boston family, and half of his regiment perished in the attack on Fort Wagner, South Carolina, in July 1863. A black butler, retired from service in the Shaw household, funded the memorial to the tune of $13,000. The 1989 film *Glory* tells the story of the regiment's heroism.

The long mall running from Beacon Street at the Joy Street entrance across the whole length of the Common to the corner of Boylston and Tremont Streets is called the Oliver Wendell Holmes Path. The eminent physician and writer recalled walking here with Amelia Lee Jackson: "I think I

A STRAND OF JEWELS

Boston Common is the first jewel in Frederick Law Olmsted's Emerald Necklace, an 1,100-acre chain of nine parks linked by parkways and waterways throughout the city. The parks include the Public Garden, Commonwealth Avenue Mall, Back Bay Fens, Riverway, Olmsted Park, Jamaica Pond Park, Arnold Arboretum, and Franklin Park. It is approximately 7 miles by foot or bicycle from the Common to Franklin Park.

The Robert Gould Shaw and Fifty-fourth Regiment Memorial attests to a battle of strength and courage. COURTESY OF THE GREATER BOSTON CONVENTION & VISITORS BUREAU

tried to speak twice without making myself distinctly audible. At last I got out the question—Will you take the long path with me?—Certainly,—said the schoolmistress,—with much pleasure—Think,—I said,—before you answer; if you take the long path with me now, I shall interpret it that we are to part no more. She answered softly, I will walk the long path with you!"

Many prominent and notable characters have walked the paths since. Walt Whitman and Ralph Waldo Emerson walked together for two hours on May 12, 1863, while the Sage of Concord used all of his powers of persuasion, without success, to convince Whitman to delete "The Children of Adam" portion of *Leaves of Grass*.

In the 1600s no one strolled the Common on Sunday; it was a day reserved for serious churchgoing. Today, Sunday is

ONE OF BOSTON'S FIRSTS

Rev. William Blackstone already lived on the slope of Beacon Hill when the Puritans arrived in Boston. Having remained in the New World after the failed Gorges expedition, the reverend was enjoying his solitude with his many books for company. Once his new neighbors settled, however, Rev. Blackstone, tired of having so much company and not tolerant of the unyielding Puritan view of life, withheld six acres at the top of the hill and sold the rest of his homestead to the town in 1634. Blackstone resettled about 35 miles away on a hill overlooking what is today the Blackstone River. He later went on to become good friends with Roger Williams and regularly spoke at his church in Providence, Rhode Island. Blackstone died in 1675 at the age of eighty. His homestead was burned down during King Philip's War and was never rebuilt.

the Common's day to shine. Easter Sunday especially finds Boston families strutting their finery on the Common. And on warm summer days, strolling the Common offers relief from the city's parched pavement. Office workers enjoy picnic lunches here. Retirees relax on benches. Children splash in Frog Pond in summer and ice-skate in winter. Year-round, people hand-feed friendly pigeons and squirrels.

History meets modern convenience beneath the park's pastoral setting, where there's a 1,300-car parking garage, and at the corner of Park and Tremont Streets is the entrance to the oldest subway in America. This corner has also been the site of memorable events, including the world's largest craps game, during the Boston police strike of 1919, and Vietnam War protests. The tradition continues, and the Common remains a popular spot for soapbox orators, who provide entertaining street theater with their passionate commentary.

SITE OF THE LIBERTY TREE
Washington and Essex Streets

A few blocks off the Freedom Trail, at the corner of Washington and Essex Streets, a plaque (high on a building) marks the place where the Patriots' famed Liberty Tree once stood.

The Liberty Tree played a pivotal role in the colonists' fight for independence when it was chosen as the tree from which to hang an effigy of poor Thomas Oliver, the Royal stamp collector. The Stamp Act was levied by the British Parliament in 1765 to help defray the cost of defending the American frontier. It taxed newspapers and various official and legal documents.

The colonists interpreted this tax as a flagrant example of taxation without representation, and Boston was in an uproar. At daybreak on August 14, members of the Sons of Liberty hanged poor Oliver in effigy.

Word of the "hanging" spread, and soon thousands of people gathered at the spot to express their admiration and approval. At dusk the crowd took down the effigy, placed it on a funeral bier, and formed a vast torchlight procession to the stamp office, which they promptly tore apart.

After attacking the homes of various Royal officials, the mob built a bonfire and cremated the effigy. The next day the real Mr. Oliver, who was also the brother-in-law of the colony's lieutenant governor, Thomas Hutchinson, was compelled to appear under the gallows of the Liberty Tree and to renounce his duties as stamp officer.

On September 11, a plate with the inscription THE TREE OF LIBERTY was placed on the trunk, and the Sons of Liberty met here. The British, knowing what the tree meant to the colonists, continually ridiculed it. A year later, during the siege of Boston, they defiantly cut it down. A contemporary journalist reported, "After a long spell of laughing and grinning, sweating and

The Liberty Tree plaque commemorates the place where the Sons of Liberty often gathered. COURTESY OF THE BOSTONIAN SOCIETY/OLD STATE HOUSE

swearing, and foaming with malice diabolical [British soldiers] cut down a tree because it bore the name of liberty."

After having stood for more than one hundred years, witness to the birth of freedom, the tree was reduced to a stump. The patriots of Boston, however, renamed it the Liberty Stump and continued to use it as a place of assembly.

STATE HOUSE
Beacon and Park Streets

The State House, begun in 1795 and completed in 1798, is the crowning achievement of Charles Bulfinch, who also designed Connecticut's State House and was the architect for the Capitol in Washington, D.C.

After returning from an architectural tour abroad, Bulfinch submitted his design for the Massachusetts capitol in November 1787. He explained that it was "in the style of a building celebrated all over Europe," London's Somerset House on the banks of the Thames, a monumental neo-Palladian government building by Sir William Chambers. More than seven years elapsed before the design was implemented, however, and Samuel Adams and Paul Revere laid the cornerstone on July 4, 1795.

The State House originally was intended for a site on the lower part of the Common, but Bulfinch had begun to design and build handsome residences near John Hancock's mansion atop Beacon Hill, so the location was changed to this more fashionable part of town. For two and a half years, the architect supervised masons, carpenters, plasterers, carvers, painters, glaziers, and roofers. Progress was slow, expenses high; but when the State House was completed, it was praised as "the most magnificent building in the Union," a marvel of "perfect taste and proportion."

STEP TO THE SIDE, PLEASE

The center doors of the State House are opened only for governors when they depart at the end of their terms and for the President of the United States. The public should enter and leave through the side doors.

Massachusetts State House

The original redbrick facade, now enlarged by two wings, generally resembles the pavilion of Lord Somerset's house; in detail, however, it is an original neoclassical Bulfinch composition. With blind-arched windows and elegant lunettes, the building—including flanking brick pavilions—is 173 feet across the front. Ninety-four feet of this expanse are occupied by the arched brick portico that supports a magnificent Corinthian colonnade, which in turn is surmounted by a pilastered pediment.

The famous golden dome, 50 feet in diameter and 30 feet high, is a grand, dominating hemisphere. It is topped by a cupola and pinecone, symbol of the lumber industry and Maine, which at the time was part of Massachusetts. First painted lead gray, the dome was sheathed in copper in 1802 by Paul Revere and Sons. It was later painted yellow, and finally gilded with gold leaf in 1874.

Enoch Williams, a nineteenth-century travel writer, reported on the view from the dome in his *Impressions of America* for London readers. "I speak soberly and without exaggeration," he wrote. "There are few views either in the new world or the old that can be compared to this."

The interior was just as handsome. Lofty ceilings, ornamental plasterwork by Daniel Raynard, and the richly carved columns and pilasters of the principal rooms were universally admired. Portraits of Massachusetts governors now hang in the entrance hall. The Sacred Cod, a 5-foot-long pinewood fish opposite the speaker's desk in the Hall of Representatives, highlights the importance of the fishing industry in Massachusetts. Although the State House has been enlarged greatly and the interior extensively remodeled, the Bulfinch front remains intact, an authentic American temple to democracy.

After the State House was built, town fathers decided it would look more impressive without Boston's other hills

The Massachusetts State House is the crowning achievement of Boston-born architect Charles Bulfinch. COURTESY OF THE GREATER BOSTON CONVENTION & VISITORS BUREAU

around it. Mount Vernon, to the west, was used to fill the river and raise Charles Street. In 1845 Cotton Hill, on the east, was leveled and used to fill a millpond at its foot. This endeavor created eight acres of downtown land, including the site of the Court House.

By a twist of fate, the private fortune of Charles Bulfinch was sinking just as his public reputation reached its height. Committing nearly all of his wealth to an ambitious residential development known as the Tontine Crescent on Franklin Street, Bulfinch was unable to weather one of the many financial panics of the early Republic. In 1799, unwilling to see its great citizen reduced to poverty, Boston elected him chief selectman and superintendent of police. As the town's leading administrator/architect, he improved nearly every aspect of his native place, from the execution of laws and the

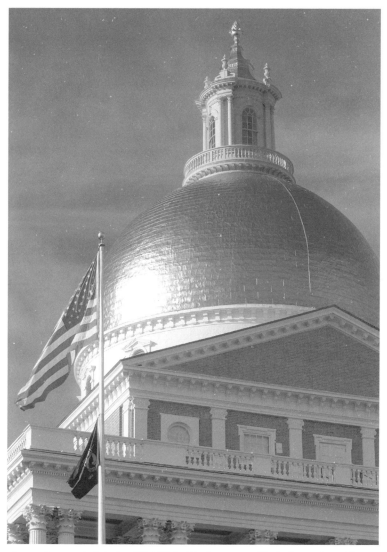

Except for a period during World War II when it was blacked out, the gold dome of the State House has gleamed for more than a century. © JO ANN SNOVER

conduct of government to the planning and laying out of new streets and the design of dozens of residential, commercial, ecclesiastical, and institutional buildings.

Given Bulfinch's lifetime of extraordinary accomplishment, it is difficult to assign preeminence to any one of his projects; and yet the State House is regarded as Bulfinch's masterpiece. In one magnificent stroke he introduced a new architecture for the new nation, powerful and majestic, expressive of the ideals embodied in the Constitution of a self-governing people. America's first professional architect set a new standard and applied it to every aspect of Boston— a legacy of excellence that endures to this day.

THE BEACON

Beacon Monument, facing Ashburton Place behind the State House, marks the highest point in Boston and pays tribute to the original monument that used to stand on Sentry Hill.

When the first settlers arrived, Boston had three hills—Sentry Hill, Mount Vernon, and Cotton Hill. On Sentry Hill, the highest, settlers erected a tall pole with rungs all the way up. On top of this lookout, they filled a pot with pitch and pinewood. In times of danger—fire or attack by Indians or the British—they set a fire to warn the inhabitants of the town. Thus the name Beacon Hill.

During the years of rebellion, the beacon blazed frequently. When the old structure blew down in 1789, the site therefore seemed appropriate for a monument "to commemorate the train of events which led to the American Revolution."

Charles Bulfinch was commissioned to design it, and it became Boston's first Revolutionary War monument. Erected in 1791, the stuccoed brick and stone monument was 60 feet tall and topped with an eagle. In 1811, however, Beacon Hill's crest was removed for landfill and the column came down.

A copy of the monument, incorporating its original tablets, was built in 1865 and stands today on the present site, where Bulfinch's vigilant eagle proudly stands guard.

The current Beacon is a memorial to the original beacon that blazed frequently during the years of rebellion in Boston.

SITE OF JOHN HANCOCK'S HOUSE

John Hancock's house, which stood on what is now the west lawn of the State House, was torn down in 1863. One of the last of the great Georgian mansions in Boston, as notable architecturally as it was historically, it was built in 1737 for John's uncle Thomas Hancock, a wealthy merchant who had started out as a bookbinder and stationer.

Two stories high and constructed of Connecticut stone brought to Boston by boat, the mansion boasted a gambrel roof, corner quoins, four large chimneys, an elegant rooftop captain's walk, and a richly paneled interior—all in all, the house of an English squire. For thirty years, until painter John Singleton Copley built his mansion, the Hancock house stood in solitary splendor among formal gardens and fruit trees on the side of old Beacon Hill, overlooking the green expanse of the Common. On Thomas's death in 1764, the estate passed to his widow. When she died in 1777, she left it to her favorite nephew, a high-living young dandy who was just beginning to espouse the cause of liberty.

Having inherited a fortune—particularly helpful to someone who was not adept at commerce—John Hancock plunged into the revolutionary politics of the day. He served as moderator of the Boston town meeting, sat as a member of the town's various rebel committees, and later became president of both the Massachusetts Revolutionary Congress and the Continental Congress in Philadelphia.

British soldiers occupied the house at the time of the signing of the Declaration of Independence, a fact that some suggest accounts for the boldness of Hancock's signature. George III had put a price on Hancock's head. When Hancock became the first signer of the Declaration of Independence, he rendered his autograph with a conspicuous flourish and declared, "John Bull can read that without spectacles! Now let him double his reward!"

Hancock served as first governor of Massachusetts, and at the end of his life he attempted to donate his house to the Commonwealth for a museum of the Revolution or a governor's mansion. The Commonwealth declined. Even after his heirs persisted, the gift was refused, and so the house was torn down. Today a plaque stands to commemorate the spot where the house once stood.

PARK STREET CHURCH

Corner of Tremont and Park Streets

The elegant Park Street Church, erected in 1809 on the site of Boston's Old Granary, dominates its streetscape; it is a masterpiece of ecclesiastical architecture and, according to American novelist Henry James, "the most interesting mass of brick and mortar in America."

Peter Banner, the church's English architect, had recently arrived in Boston from Connecticut, where he had designed buildings for Yale University. Banner drew on nearly every element of Charles Bulfinch's residential design vocabulary, infused it with the grace of Sir Christopher Wren's London spires, and produced an edifice so striking and so enduring that the Trinitarian Evangelical congregation has never left.

Although the lofty steeple was shortened after a bad spell of swaying in the nineteenth century, Park Street Church still presents an extremely graceful facade, with bowfront colonnades, a Palladian tower window, recessed arches, a pedimented belfry, a towering steeple, and carved wood detail by

17

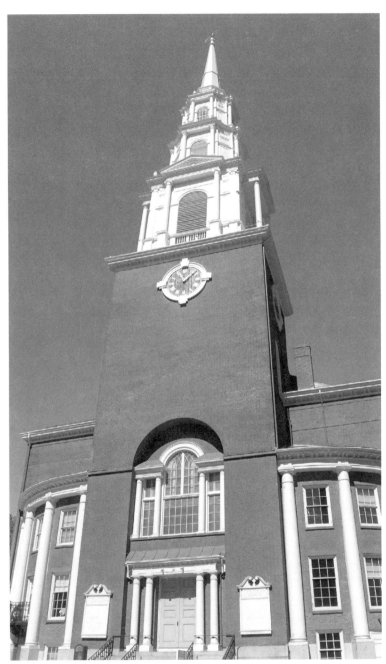

Park Street Church has been the site of many pivotal moments in Boston's history. © MARY LANE

Boston's Solomon Willard, architect of the Bunker Hill Monument.

Despite its superior commercial site in the heart of downtown Boston, the church has never been endangered by possible sale or demolition. During a period of financial difficulty, however, part of the building was rented out as a tearoom, until it was discovered that women were displeasing the Lord by smoking cigarettes!

Park Street Church is no stranger to controversy. On the Fourth of July, 1829, William Lloyd Garrison, the great abolitionist and publisher of the *Liberator,* gave his first public antislavery address—an oration not well received by his audience, who at one point tried to lynch him. And in 1849 Charles Sumner delivered his powerful oration, "The War System of Nations," to the American Peace Society.

In part as recognition of the many hellfire-and-brimstone sermons thundered from its pulpit, and in part because brimstone was stored in the church's cellar during the War of 1812, the corner of Park and Tremont Streets is known as Brimstone Corner.

FIRE AND BRIM . . . UH . . . SUBWAY?

On a Sunday morning in November 1895, as a pastor sat in his study working on a sermon, the windows suddenly came crashing in, and the clergyman found himself fighting for his life in an avalanche of mud. A workman, digging a nearby tunnel for America's first subway, had broken a huge water main. The pastor escaped, but, along with his evening sermon, the study was ruined.

That evening the minister delivered a sermon filled with righteous wrath, denouncing the subway as "an infernal hole" and suggesting that none other than Satan had been responsible for the "unchristian outrage."

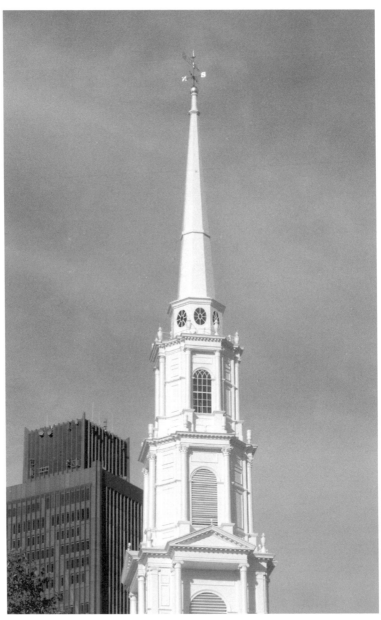

Now standing tall over Boston, Park Street Church's steeple once had to be shortened to avoid swaying. © JO ANN SNOVER

THE PLACE OF FIRSTS

The first Sunday school was organized at Park Street Church in 1818.

The first missionaries to Hawaii were dispatched from this church in 1819.

On Independence Day 1831 Samuel Francis Smith's song "America," also known as "My Country 'Tis of Thee," was first sung here.

PARK STREET CHURCH INFORMATION

HOURS: 9:30 a.m. to 3:30 p.m. Tuesday through Saturday, mid-June through August. Winter hours by appointment only. Sunday services are held year-round at 8:30 a.m., 11:00 a.m., 4:00 p.m., and 6:00 p.m.

ADMISSION: Free

PHONE: (617) 523-3383

WHEELCHAIR ACCESSIBILITY: Yes

GRANARY BURYING GROUND

Tremont Street, Near Park Street Church

> *For nearly three hundred years it has kept its hallowed*
> *peace. Its headstones are little and dull, and covered*
> *with moss. And the trees that shelter them are grim and*
> *old. And, after dark, the little night winds sob as they*
> *tiptoe through the gloom.*
>> —Eleanor Early, *This Is Boston,* 1930

The Granary Burying Ground was laid out in 1660 as the Old South Burying Ground on land that was part of Boston Common. "There is a lovely solemnity about this little cemetery," noted Eleanor Early in her 1930 book, *This Is Boston.* The cemetery takes its name from the ugly wooden building erected in 1737 to store wheat and other grains for distribution to the poor. Since the granary was torn down and the beautiful Park Street Church was erected in its place, the church's lithe lines provide contrast to the Burying Ground's heavily symbolic granite gate with its winged globe and downturned torches.

More than 1,600 graves are located here. In addition to ordinary men, women, and children who pioneered the little world of Boston, scores of Revolutionary War soldiers; the city's first mayor, John Phillips; and the five Boston Massacre victims are buried here. This is also the final resting place of three signers of the Declaration of Independence—John Hancock, Samuel Adams, and Robert Treat Paine—along with nine governors; philanthropist Peter Faneuil, "Funel" on his flat stone; diarist Judge Samuel Sewall, who lived to repent his part in the witchcraft trials; Paul Revere; and Benjamin Franklin's parents, whose graves are marked with the

This obelisk guards the graves of Benjamin Franklin's parents.

original stone and an obelisk erected in 1827 by the citizens of Boston.

Among old graveyards with their illustrious dead, their quaint inscriptions, and above all their sense of repose, Granary

THERE WAS AN OLD WOMAN . . .

Among the markers in the Granary Burying Ground is the 1690 stone of Mary Goose, who, although a mother, was not Mother Goose. That literary distinction belongs to the second wife of Isaac Goose, Elizabeth, who had charge of so many children (twenty) that it is perfectly possible she did not know what to do. For the entire story visit www.celebrateboston.com/literature/mothergoose/mothergoose.htm.

Burying Ground is unsurpassed. Many seventeenth-century stones still stand, richly lettered and carved with ghastly death's heads and emblems of the fruits of paradise, Puritan symbols of the departing soul and the blissful eternity that is its destination. The oldest marker in the cemetery belongs to Hannah Allen; the oldest upright stone, to John Wakefield.

The burying ground harbors some lesser-known but interesting characters, too. Ann Pollard, a child when she arrived with the first settlers, was the first to hop ashore at Shawmutt, later known as Boston. She grew up, married, and gave birth to numerous children. Surviving her husband by decades, she followed an independent, pipe-smoking course and operated the wild-and-woolly Horse Shoe Tavern. At the age of 103, she had her portrait painted. When she died two years later, the whole town joined her hundred-plus descendants in mourning her.

Benjamin Woodbridge found his way into this resting place in 1728. He made an injudicious remark at the Royal Exchange, the merchants' gathering place, and was challenged to a duel with swords. He accepted. The affair of honor, held on Boston Common, ended with a rapier running through the twenty-year-old.

The story of Elisha Brown is etched on his stone. During the British occupation of Boston, he single-handedly prevented an entire regiment of His Majesty's troops from dispossessing him of his spacious home, which they coveted as a barracks. Years later he died a peaceful death in that home.

GRANARY BURYING GROUND INFORMATION

HOURS: 9:00 a.m. to 5:00 p.m. daily

ADMISSION: Free

PHONE: Boston Parks Department, (617) 635-4504

WHEELCHAIR ACCESSIBILITY: Limited; four steps to enter in front, but side gate (off Beacon Street) has ramp

PLEASE, NO GRAVE RUBBINGS.

KING'S CHAPEL AND BURYING GROUND

58 Tremont Street

This chapel ended up as something quite different than what its controversial beginnings would have indicated. It began in 1688, when, after townsfolk refused to sell him land, the despotic Royal Governor, Sir Edmund Andros, appropriated a corner of the Puritan town's first graveyard for a small wood chapel, complete with spire, to house the first Anglican congregation in North America.

Sentiment against Andros had been building, and this affront provoked such strong hostility from the colonists that he was forced to flee. But King's Chapel remained. Royal officials continued to worship in handsome style, surrounded

The Ionic columns of King's Chapel's portico look like granite but are actually wood. © 2005 CITY MAPS INC.

by opulent decoration. Before the church was built, William and Mary had presented the communion table and chancel tables, still in use. Dukes and earls donated silver service. Queen Anne and King George III also favored the church with gifts of silver and vestments.

The congregation grew, and in 1710 the building was enlarged. By 1741 Boston's Anglicans had decided to replace the old wood chapel with a London-style stone edifice, but the project was deferred until 1748, when funds were raised. The congregation retained the talents of Peter Harrison, a gentleman designer from Newport, Rhode Island.

Harrison's final design called for a substantial stone building and tower, to be lightened by the "beautiful effect" of a lofty wood steeple. He also proposed a double row of windows, the lower smaller than the upper, causing one wit to comment that he "had heard of the Cannons of the Church, but had never before seen the portholes."

When Governor William Shirley laid the cornerstone for the new edifice in August 1749, angry Puritans threw garbage. Nevertheless, great blocks of rough-hewn stone walls soon rose around the chapel, which was used until 1753. Then it was demolished and thrown out the windows of its successor.

Because money ran out, the "beautiful effect" of Peter Harrison's steeple was never realized. Yet the interior of the new church was a marvel of Georgian elegance and home to New England's first church organ. When the building was completed in 1754, the Anglicans were pleased.

During the siege of Boston, British military and naval officers worshiped here. With the hasty departure of the Tories, Boston removed the King from the chapel and rechristened it Stone Chapel. The name didn't last.

In 1790, shortly after George Washington attended an oratorio, the colonnaded portico was added. The final change took place in 1785, when the first Episcopal church in New England became the first Unitarian church in America. The congregation, however, summoned by Paul Revere's bell, still uses the Anglican *Book of Common Prayer.*

KING'S CHAPEL BURYING GROUND, TREMONT STREET

For thirty years this was the town's only burying ground. In September 1630 Sir Isaac Johnson, a leader of the Massachusetts Bay Company, succumbed to the rigors of the New World and was buried in the southwest corner of his garden lot. As other Puritans planned for their demises, they asked to be buried alongside Brother Johnson.

King's Chapel Burying Ground is the final resting place of nearly the entire first generation of Boston's English settlers. The oldest gravestone in Boston, William Paddy's 1658 marker, is found here. The Massachusetts Bay Colony's first governor, John Winthrop; William Dawes, who accompanied Paul Revere on his midnight ride; and Elizabeth Pain, the model for Nathaniel Hawthorne's Hester Prynne in *The Scarlet Letter,* are interred here, too. Mary Chilton, who arrived with the Pilgrims on the *Mayflower* and was the first Englishwoman to set foot in New England, is here, too, as are the pastors of the First Church and other early notables. After the Episcopal church was erected on the corner, Royal Governor William Shirley and other Tory officials, along with British soldiers, were interred here, as well.

The present arrangement of the headstones is the work of an old-time superintendent of burials. He apparently considered the beautifully carved old slates to be elements of a composition (his), rather than accurate grave markers. Perhaps this is why the old First Graveyard, or King's Chapel Burying Ground, is replete with legends of ghostly doings and supernatural restlessness.

BENJAMIN FRANKLIN'S STATUE

Old City Hall Grounds, 45 School Street

Erected in 1856, this 8-foot-tall bronze likeness of Benjamin Franklin by Richard S. Greenough is Boston's first public portrait statue. In executing the commission, the sculptor observed that he "found the left of the great man's face philosophical and reflective, and the right side funny and smiling." Tablets on the base recall scenes from Franklin's life.

The statue is located in front of Boston's Old City Hall, an ornate edifice built in 1862 in the French Second Empire style, which seems particularly appropriate since Franklin served as this country's first ambassador to France.

On the sidewalk in front of the statue, *City Carpet,* a mosaic by Lilli Ann Killen Rosenberg, marks the original site

This memorial to Benjamin Franklin is Boston's first public portrait statue.

of Boston Latin School, the first public school in America. Brass letters, Venetian glass, and ceramic pieces spell out the names of its famous alumni, including Samuel Adams, Cotton Mather, and John Hancock. Franklin received his few years of formal schooling and a taste for books at Boston Latin School, sometimes called the Free Writing School, which opened in 1635 and established a standard of excellence that continues at its home on Avenue Louis Pasteur.

Largely self-taught, Franklin excelled as a printer, writer, editor, inventor, scientist, military officer, politician, and statesman. He is the only American who signed all four of the critical documents in Revolutionary-era history: the Declaration of Independence, the Treaty of Alliance with France, the treaty of peace with Great Britain, and the Constitution of the United States.

THE OLD CORNER BOOKSTORE

3 School Street, Corner of Washington Street

In 1712, a year after fire had destroyed the neighborhood, Thomas Crease built this solid brick house as his residence and Boston's first apothecary shop. With its steep gambrel

A GLASS OF RED?

In the mid-1800s, which could be considered the Golden Age of American Literature, the former Crease house was the country's literary heart, an informal clubhouse where writers could always find good conversation and a glass of claret. Here, too, the famous Saturday Club was born. Its members were the backbone of the house magazine, the *Atlantic Monthly*. James Fields was the magazine's second editor.

The Old Corner Bookstore stands at the corner of School and Washington Streets and has for almost 300 years. COURTESY OF THE BOSTONIAN SOCIETY/OLD STATE HOUSE

roof, brick belt courses, and corner quoins, the English-style town house was one of the handsomest in the community of about 10,000 people.

The Crease house became a bookshop in the 1820s, when the building was acquired by William D. Ticknor. A resourceful young man, he obtained the rights to publish works of British authors by adopting the then novel practice of paying royalties. In 1833 Ticknor took in as partner James T. Fields, a book clerk who astonished his colleagues by correctly predicting, as soon as they entered the shop, what books customers would buy.

BANISHED!

In the 1600s, the land on which Crease built his house almost a century later belonged to William Hutchinson. Hutchinson's brilliant wife, Anne, ministered to the sick and held informal discussion groups for women in her home. Her controversial religious teachings challenged the male clergy and led to a dangerous Puritan schism, so in 1634 the General Court (the Massachusetts legislature) banished her from the colony. Anne Hutchinson took her husband and fourteen children first to Rhode Island with Roger Williams, then to Pelham, New York, where, except for one daughter, all were killed by Indians.

Fields was instrumental in helping the company to sign contracts with New England authors, and from 1833 to 1864 Ticknor and Fields, Inc., was the country's leading publisher. Its authors included Henry Wadsworth Longfellow, Harriet Beecher Stowe, Nathaniel Hawthorne, Ralph Waldo Emerson, John Greenleaf Whittier, Oliver Wendell Holmes, and Henry David Thoreau. *Walden* and "The Battle Hymn of the Republic" were published here.

After Ticknor and Fields moved out, the building housed a number of different booksellers. By the mid-twentieth century, it had become a pizza parlor in a prime location for a new parking garage. With encouragement from the city and financial assistance from the Boston Globe Newspaper Company, Historic Boston, Inc., purchased the building in 1960 and restored it to its original appearance. Today Historic Boston conducts its citywide preservation efforts in upstairs office space.

SITE OF FRANKLIN'S PRINT SHOP

Court Street

A bronze tablet on the facade of the building at 17 Court Street marks the place where Benjamin Franklin was apprenticed to his brother. James had gone to London to learn "the art or mystery" of printing, a rare calling in New England. Upon his return, he established a print shop and, in 1721, launched a newspaper, the *New-England Courant*.

James Franklin was a good printer, and, as a newspaperman, he possessed a sure sense of what his readers wanted to know. Young Ben's sprightly writing under the byline "Mrs. Silence Dogood" also contributed to the paper's success. Indeed, the *New-England Courant* soon put the competition, the *Boston News-Letter,* out of business.

Ben set the type by hand; absorbed the literary and political influences of the newspaper office and pressroom; and printed books, broadsides, and circulars, all of which he hawked on the street. He obtained the best informal education a hardworking printer's devil could hope for.

This artist's rendering shows what Franklin's print shop might have looked like in the 1700s.

"In a little time," he wrote, "I made great proficiency in the business, and became a useful hand." In addition to his duties as typesetter, pressman, and newsboy, young Ben wrote some topical verse that was published in broadside form.

James's ability to reflect his townspeople's real interests and opinions, however, gave offense to the conservative legislature, and the Massachusetts General Court imprisoned him for a month. Ben ran the newspaper during his brother's absence and continued, as he put it, "to give our rulers some rubs in it." After James was released with the injunction he not print the *Courant,* the paper was published in Benjamin's name.

Eventually the brothers had a falling-out. James was an abusive brother and master. Ben bitterly resented him and later wrote, "His harsh and tyrannical treatment of me [was] a means of impressing me with that aversion to arbitrary power that has stuck to me thro' my whole life."

Armed with a love of politics and writing, the self-reliant seventeen-year-old secured a release from his indenture and booked passage on a boat bound for Philadelphia. From there he traveled to London, where he published his "Dissertation on Liberty and Necessity, Pleasure and Pain." By 1726 he was back in Philadelphia, writing tracts and publishing his own newspaper. In 1732 he began the witty and worldly *Poor Richard's Almanac,* which helped to define the newly emerging American character: industrious, practical, and optimistic.

Travelers who have experienced unwelcome interrogation by strangers can appreciate the impatience of the peripatetic Franklin. Weary of nosy tavern keepers who pumped guests for the latest news, he cut off their attempts at conversation with a set response. "My name is Benjamin Franklin," he would say. "I was born in Boston. I am a printer by profession

SITE OF BENJAMIN FRANKLIN'S BIRTHPLACE, 17 MILK STREET

A bronze bust of Ben Franklin on the second story at 17 Milk Street, the Boston Post Building, commemorates the site where Franklin was born on January 17, 1706.

His father, Josiah Franklin, an English dyer, arrived in Boston in 1682. After the death of his first wife, Josiah married Abiah Foulger of Nantucket and entered into the messy and malodorous business of soap boiling. He was a tallow chandler, or maker and seller of candles.

In 1691 the elder Franklin had a family home built on Milk Street. His youngest son, the fifteenth of his seventeen children, was born here and christened Benjamin Franklin.

Fire destroyed the modest wood-frame house in 1810.

Benjamin Franklin's birthplace, which no longer stands but is commemorated with a bronze bust of the great man.

and am traveling to Philadelphia. I shall have to return at such and such a time, and I have no news. Now what can you give me for dinner?"

Although Franklin is associated with his adopted state of Pennsylvania, Massachusetts proudly claims him as a native son. In 1778 the Commonwealth named a town in honor of the statesman, scholar, and humanist. To show his appreciation, Franklin considered giving his namesake either a church bell or a collection of books. Finally he decided on books. His reason, he said, was that "sense [is] more essential than sound."

OLD SOUTH
MEETING HOUSE

310 Washington Street, Corner of Milk Street

The Old South Meeting House stands on the site of the Puritans' original meetinghouse, a place of worship built in 1669 for dissenters from the First Church. They had sought a more liberal policy for church membership, and the first meetinghouse was a typical Puritan structure, severe in its lines and devoid of a steeple or anything else that might give the appearance of a church.

To the Puritans a church was a building in which the rites of the Church of England were observed. They had broken from that church and its "popish" liturgy. In their eyes a plain, barnlike meetinghouse was as acceptable to God as any cathedral in Christendom.

TEA ANYONE?

The largest and most famous assembly occurred at the Old South Meeting House on the afternoon of December 16, 1773, when thousands of people crowded into the meetinghouse and thronged the streets outside to hear Sam Adams orate on the nonimportation of certain British goods, particularly those to be found in the holds of three recently arrived merchant vessels.

After Adams, Josiah Quincy spoke. He recognized in the meeting attendants' outrage and the governor's intransigence the makings of a mighty tempest. "I see the clouds which now rise thick and fast upon the horizon," Quincy declared. "The thunders roll and the lightnings play, and to the God who rides on the whirlwind and directs the storm I commit my country!" The crowd responded with a mighty whoop, and off it surged, torches blazing, to the waterfront for an evening tea party.

The Old South Meeting House was frequently used for mass gatherings and public meetings, some more controversial than others. © 2005 CITY MAPS INC.

Two generations of prosperity and theological evolution, and a by-then fashionable congregation, resulted in a new house of worship being built in the latest style. The Third Religious Society razed the old building in 1729. In its place they erected the present Georgian structure with brick laid in Flemish bond.

Josiah Blanchard's massive building features Palladian windows, a tower, a 180-foot wooden steeple, a belfry, and a two-tier gallery. Negro slaves—including Phillis Wheatley, America's first black woman author—sat in the topmost tier of the gallery. Although the congregation persisted in calling it a meetinghouse, the building was and is unmistakably a church, Boston's second oldest, and a model for much colonial ecclesiastical architecture.

By the middle of the eighteenth century, Boston, a prosperous English city, had a population of 25,000. In these years the Old South Meeting House was frequently used for mass gatherings and town meetings too large to fit into Faneuil Hall—some more controversial than others. And right up to the outbreak of the Revolution, Old South served as a rebel auditorium as well as a place of worship. Because no other structure in Boston was so readily identified with the patriotic cause, the British took special revenge here.

WHERE THERE'S A WILL . . .

One evening, Dr. Joseph Warren, the handsome, aristocratic physician who later died at Bunker Hill, was prevented from entering the Old South Meeting House. Not to be deterred, the young rebel climbed over the heads of British soldiers, through a second-story window in back, and addressed the patriots inside. His daring so humiliated the British that he became a marked man.

From June 1774 to June 1776, the years during which the Redcoats occupied Boston, Old South was used as an officers' club and a riding academy, with a liquor dispensary in the gallery. The pulpit was torn down; the high box floor was broken up for kindling. In the large open area thus created, several tons of dirt were dumped and raked smooth. Where the word of God and of man had rung out, the Queen's Light Dragoons spurred their mounts round and round, sometimes to drunken applause from the gallery above.

After the British were expelled from Boston, the congregation returned to its meetinghouse and restored the interior to its former state, including candlelight chandeliers and a white pulpit. The people of the town continued to hold overflow meetings here. The only lasting effect of the British presence was the loss of many valuable documents, including the manuscript of Pilgrim Governor William Bradford's *History of Plymouth*. Some fifty years later, however, the priceless documents were accidentally discovered in England. A letter from George Washington to his dentist, thanking him for a set of artificial teeth, was returned and is kept in the Old South Meeting House's safe.

Twice Old South has nearly gone up in smoke. In December 1810 the roof caught fire, and the building seemed doomed. Fortunately the efforts of a courageous mastmaker, Isaac Harris, proved equal to the task. In gratitude for his extraordinary rooftop exertions, the Third Religious Society presented him with an elegant silver water pitcher, which is now on display in the Museum of Fine Arts.

Old South was threatened again in 1872, when the greatest of all the city's fires destroyed sixty-five acres of downtown Boston. Only judicious dynamiting of nearby structures halted the conflagration just short of Old South. Afterward Old South was pressed into service in a new role, as a temporary post office.

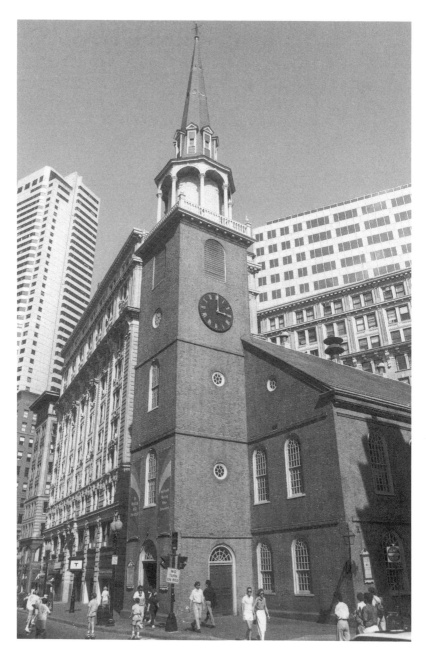

The Old South Meeting House still stands proud after facing many threats in its almost 300 years of existence.

Preserved from the ravages of fire, the Old South Meeting House soon faced demolition in the name of progress. After bitter debate in 1875, the congregation built a new Old South in the Back Bay and put its former home up for sale.

The noble old building, located on a valuable commercial site, seemed destined for the wrecker's ball. Boston authors Ralph Waldo Emerson, Julia Ward Howe, and Louisa May Alcott successfully campaigned to stop the demolition. In a remarkable burst of civic pride, Bostonians formed an Old South Association. In short order they raised the $400,000 purchase price—the first instance of urban historical preservation in America.

The association continues to maintain Old South as a museum. Its venerable walls reverberate with the sounds of meetings, lectures, plays, concerts, memorial services, and church services. It is a living monument to the days and deeds of Otis, Adams, Quincy, and others who forged a new nation.

OLD SOUTH MEETING HOUSE INFORMATION

HOURS: 9:30 a.m. to 5:00 p.m. April 1 through October 31; 10:00 a.m. to 4:00 p.m. November 1 through March 31; closed Thanksgiving, Christmas Eve, Christmas Day, New Year's Day

ADMISSION: Adults, $5; senior citizens and students, $4; ages six to eighteen, $1

PHONE: (617) 482-6439

WEB SITE: www.oldsouthmeetinghouse.org

WHEELCHAIR ACCESSIBILITY: Yes

OLD STATE HOUSE

206 Washington Street

The Old State House, built in 1713, is the oldest surviving public building in Boston. It served as the capitol of the colonial British government before becoming home to the Massachusetts Assembly, the most radical of the colonial legislatures, and was the setting for George Washington's triumphal 1789 return to Boston, as well as for the inauguration of the Commonwealth of Massachusetts's first governor, John Hancock.

Over the years it has had many incarnations—firehouse, city hall, courthouse, newspaper office, museum. While we do not know the name of the architect of this handsome red-brick building, two-and-a-half stories high and surmounted by a cupola, we do know that the present structure rose like a phoenix from the ashes of an earlier building.

The original Town House had been the gift of Captain Robert Keayne, an English tailor who became America's first self-made millionaire. The Puritans denounced him for "making too much profit" and forced him to confess publicly his "covetous and corrupt heart."

When Keayne died, however, his will included bequests to shelter "the country people that come with their provisions" and to provide a meeting place for merchants, an armory for the

---

HAIL TO THE QUEEN

When Queen Elizabeth II visited Boston during our nation's bicentennial, she chose to address Americans from the balcony of Great Britain's former Town House, a building adorned with the lion and unicorn, symbols of the British Crown. Perhaps she was not aware that the first public reading to the Bostonians of the Declaration of Independence from Great Britain took place from that balcony on July 18, 1776, a custom repeated every July 4 since.

The Old State House has had many uses and has played a great role in Boston's history. COURTESY OF THE GREATER BOSTON CONVENTION & VISITORS BUREAU artillery company, a library for the learned, and a chamber for the legislature. Accordingly the first Town House was erected in 1657 at the intersection of the city's two main thoroughfares, King Street and the Road to the Neck, now State and Washington Streets. It was the middle of an open-air marketplace where all of Boston purchased its food and met to gossip. The Old State House was dedicated to the use of the Massachusetts General Court and the Royal government with its various Courts of Justice. Here the government conducted the business of the province and tried and decided colonial cases.

The colony's business did not, though, run smoothly. Inevitably the General Court and the Royal government clashed. In 1692 the king, alarmed by a growing independence of spirit in Massachusetts, appointed a Royal Governor to the colony. Still, the colony's representative assembly refused to be ruled. Indeed, by the 1720s the General Court had come to resent the governor's authority to such an extent that it refused to pay his salary.

In turn, the governor challenged the powers of the legislature by suspending its privileges. Over the years governors came and governors went, and the representatives of the people of Massachusetts continued their struggle for power.

Occasionally citizens expressed themselves directly. In 1747 a mob, incensed by the Royal Navy's drafting of Americans, marched on the Town House and shattered its windows. To restore order, Governor William Shirley came out on the balcony and delivered a conciliatory speech.

In 1748 flames gutted the Town House, which was quickly rebuilt and restored to its former elegance. Throughout the 1760s liberty's spokesmen used these halls to voice their opposition to British policy. Here John Adams and John Hancock inspired their peers. And here James Otis delivered his impassioned, four-hour speech on the sanctity of individual rights, provoking John Adams to remark, "Then and there, the child Independence was born."

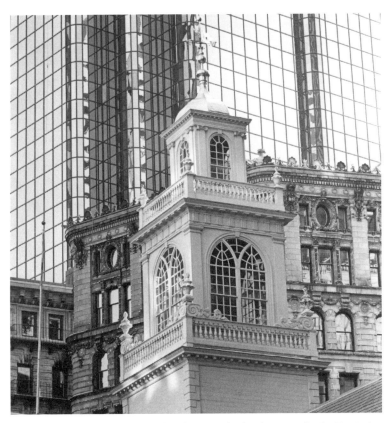

The Old State House stands tall and now is the headquarters for the Bostonian Society and its museum. COURTESY OF THE BOSTONIAN SOCIETY/OLD STATE HOUSE

By 1774 the Massachusetts legislature had become a rebel congress, disbanded by the Crown. Members fled British-held Boston and regrouped in Salem. One year later, after the evacuation of the Redcoats from Boston, the Old State House again became the seat of government, this time the independent government of the Commonwealth of Massachusetts. It was rechristened with a large American eagle adorning its western facade.

Despite its stirring history, the Old State House fell on hard times. In 1881 city fathers were undecided about its utility. Some, on learning that the commercial value of the site was $1.5 million, urged the building's demolition, whereupon the city of Chicago offered to purchase it for reerection on the shores of Lake Michigan. The plan was so inimical to Bostonians that the historic edifice was immediately given a complete restoration.

Today, as the headquarters of the Bostonian Society and its museum, the Old State House retains dignity amid the skyscrapers of the new Boston.

OLD STATE HOUSE INFORMATION

HOURS: 9:00 a.m. to 5:00 p.m. daily, except Thanksgiving, Christmas, and New Year's Day; extended hours in the summer

ADMISSION: Adults, $5; senior citizens and students over age eighteen, $4; children ages six to eighteen, $1

PHONE: (617) 720-1713

WHEELCHAIR ACCESSIBILITY: Lift available

SITE OF THE BOSTON MASSACRE

Congress and State Streets

Beneath the east balcony of the Old State House, a star within a ring of cobblestones marks the site of the first blood shed in the American Revolution.

In October 1768 British troops invaded and occupied Boston. It was a provocative move, escalating the tensions that had come to characterize relations between the Crown and the colony. The Crown had sought to enforce one restrictive act after another, while Bostonians had persistently and sometimes violently defied British authority. Having met with such firm opposition and noncompliance, Royal officials feared an outright insurrection.

In fact, the presence of Redcoats only spurred the Sons of Liberty to greater resistance. For two years the town smoldered, until, in the summer of 1769, Royal Governor Francis Bernard fled to England. Effective regular government came to an end.

By 1770 Bostonians were openly clashing with the Redcoats. Armed conflict seemed inevitable. On the evening of March 5, a band of townsmen goaded two soldiers into a fight, then thrashed them. Fearing reprisal, they sounded the alarm for general action. Bells pealed and people poured into the streets. A crowd gathered in Town House Square in front of the Old State House and surrounded a lone British sentinel.

Soon British troops arrived. The mob turned abusive, waving clubs and threatening bloody murder. People pelted soldiers with snowballs and rocks. They taunted the soldiers, calling out, "come out, you rascals, you bloody-backs, you lobster scoundrels—fire if you dare. God damn you, fire and be damned!"

Scorned and reviled, the soldiers stood in fear of their lives. After one of them was walloped with a stick, he broke down and fired. The rest followed suit, discharging their muskets point-blank at their tormentors.

The mob scattered. But three men lay dead, including Crispus Attucks, the first African American to die for the patriot cause. Of the eight wounded the townsfolk carried away that night, two later died of their injuries. Blood had been shed. The Sons of Liberty had martyrs, and Boston would never be the same.

The sight of the Redcoats in Boston preyed on the citizens' already fraying nerves. COURTESY OF THE GREATER BOSTON CONVENTION & VISITORS BUREAU

The countryside erupted. Minutemen prepared to march on Boston and drive the British into the sea. Wholesale slaughter was averted only because Redcoat regiments withdrew to a fort in the harbor and surrendered the soldiers. At the trial, John Adams and Josiah Quincy defended the soldiers. Though all but two were acquitted of manslaughter, the Boston Massacre ever afterward served as a rallying point for the patriot cause.

Every March 5, the event is commemorated with an oration lest Bostonians forget the night "our streets were stained with the Blood of our Brethren, our ears were wounded by the groans of the dying, and our eyes were tormented with the sight of the mangled bodies of the Dead."

President John Adams later declared, "On that night, the foundation of American independence was laid."

FANEUIL HALL
Dock Square

Faneuil Hall once dominated Boston's waterfront. From 1742, when New York–born merchant Peter Faneuil presented his adopted community with the elegant market, until 1825, when Boston filled in the old Town Dock area to meet demands for more market space, the handsome redbrick building welcomed trading ships into a port bustling with business.

LISTEN A SPELL

Historical talks are given at Faneuil Hall daily every half hour on the half hour, 9:30 a.m. to 4:30 p.m., except when the hall is being used for special events.

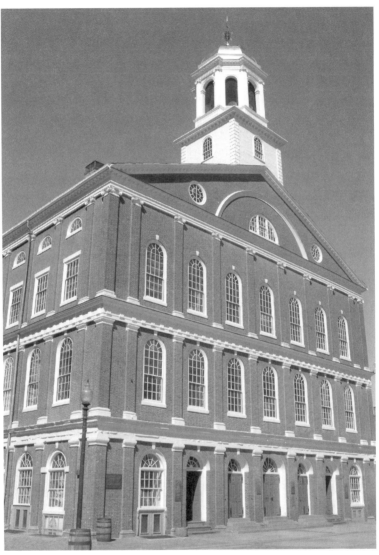

Faneuil Hall is now much farther away from the waterfront than it used to be.
© MARY LANE

But Peter Faneuil was no sober-sided businessman. He had inherited most of his money from his uncle Andrew after promising that he would never marry. He honored the promise and enjoyed a reputation as "the Jolly Bachelor of Boston." He even christened one of his ships the *Jolly Bachelor*.

Faneuil proposed a central market building as a remedy for the "disadvantage under which trade was conducted with no market house as a center of exchange." Over the years similar proposals had been defeated. Prosperous shipping merchants, who would benefit from such a facility, supported Faneuil, while peddlers and street hawkers, wary of competition, opposed him. To garner greater support for his central market, Faneuil added a second-floor town hall. A compromise was reached when authorities allowed Faneuil to build the market at his own expense and donate it to the city.

In the years leading up to the Revolutionary War, the town hall reverberated with tumultuous meetings and midnight assemblies. James Otis, one of the fomenters of the American Revolution, may have dubbed it "Cradle of Liberty." Here Boston's orators thundered their dissent from the Navigation Acts, the Intolerable Acts, and all other acts of the Crown that would restrict the traditional rights and privileges of New England. Here the citizens of the New World claimed the rights of free men. Here, too, Sam Adams, the foremost Son of Liberty, led the town meeting to vote its adamant "opposition to Tyrants and their Minions."

CONTROVERSY NO STRANGER

The first of the meetings on tea was held at Faneuil Hall on November 5, 1773. John Hancock and other Bostonians met to discuss the fate of that "baneful weed." Famous abolitionists Frederick Douglass, Wendell Phillips, and William Lloyd Garrison all spoke here as well.

Oratory begot direct and sometimes reckless action. One night in 1765 a well-liquored crowd, infuriated by enforcement of the Stamp Act, gathered at Faneuil Hall by the light of a bonfire and attacked the homes of Crown officials. In their frenzy they even tore apart the governor's mansion.

After a fire destroyed the building in 1762, it was quickly rebuilt. In 1805 Charles Bulfinch, the first professional architect in the United States, enlarged and modified the building. Bulfinch doubled the size of the original 40-by-100-foot structure but retained and repeated the Doric and Tuscan pilasters and arched windows of portrait painter John Smibert's original design. He added a spacious third story of his own composition and repositioned the cupola and grasshopper weathervane.

Peter Faneuil himself had chosen the famous gilded grasshopper with the green glass eye to crown his gift to the city. He borrowed the symbol of finance from London, where Martin's Bank and the Royal Exchange were topped by grasshopper vanes. The grasshopper is now so strongly associated with Boston, however, that an American consul once tested citizens claiming to be residents of the city by asking them to identify the most renowned weathervane in the United States.

On November 7, 1960, the eve of the presidential election, John F. Kennedy, ever mindful of historical significance, wound up his campaign with a speech at Faneuil Hall.

Faneuil Hall still serves as a handsome mercantile land-mark, but more than that, Faneuil Hall holds a special niche in history and in Boston as a place of public meeting. It is the centerpiece of a scene fully as busy and as colorful as in the days of merchant shipping and revolutionary zeal.

FANEUIL HALL INFORMATION

HOURS: 9:00 a.m. to 5:00 p.m. daily, except when a meeting is being held; closed Thanksgiving, Christmas, and New Year's Day

ADMISSION: Free

PHONE: (617) 242-5642

WHEELCHAIR ACCESSIBILITY: Elevator

QUINCY MARKET

Opposite Faneuil Hall

In 1823, one year after Boston became a city, Josiah Quincy, who had served Massachusetts as a congressman in Washing-ton, was elected mayor for the first of what would be five terms.

The dynamic Quincy (1772–1864), later president of Harvard College, greatly improved municipal services. Dur-ing his tenure he established a standard of service for cities everywhere. He instituted a system for cleaning streets, improved education, and reorganized the police force and fire department. Then he turned his attention to improving and enlarging Boston's limited market facilities "without great expense to the city."

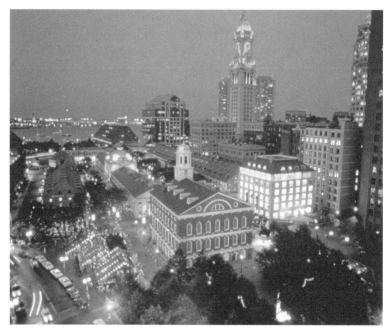

Today, Quincy Market serves as an inspiration to old cities everywhere that aspire to revive their downtown areas. COURTESY OF THE GREATER BOSTON CONVENTION & VISITORS BUREAU

Braving widespread doubt and criticism, the resourceful mayor ordered a landfill of the stagnant waters near the Town Dock. Where wharf rats had scurried, there arose a central marketplace designed by the progressive Boston architect Alexander Parris. The huge two-story building (50 by 535 feet), with its Greek porticoes and domed central pavilion, was constructed in 1825 of granite from the quarries of Quincy, Massachusetts.

The project took one year, and sale of the newly created real estate paid for the entire project. Moreover, the brick warehouses that flanked the market and other structures that were built on the six new streets increased the tax base and filled the city's coffers.

Today Quincy Marketplace, redeveloped by James Rouse, constitutes one of the finest urban shopping and dining areas in the world. It serves as an inspiration to old cities everywhere that aspire to revive their downtown areas.

QUINCY MARKET INFORMATION

HOURS: 10:00 a.m. to 9:00 p.m. Monday through Saturday; noon to 6:00 p.m. Sunday. Extended hours for the food colonnade.

ADMISSION: Free

PHONE: (617) 338-2323

WHEELCHAIR ACCESSIBILITY: Yes

BOSTON TEA PARTY SHIPS AND MUSEUM

Congress Street Bridge; Fort Point Channel

At press time this site was undergoing extensive renovation. It is scheduled to reopen to the public in the summer of 2009. The *Beaver*, the *Dartmouth*, and the *Eleanor* are replicas of the three British vessels that sailed into Boston Harbor in November 1773, carrying cargoes of East India Company tea.

Just the previous month the rebellious colonies had agreed to prevent the British company from docking its ships and selling its tea on American shores. They were determined not to pay the tea tax. Indeed, many colonists had stopped drinking tea altogether rather than pay the tax, the last vestige of the hated Townshend Revenue Bill, which Parliament had enacted in 1767 to tax goods the colonists imported.

The colonists had refused to purchase taxed commodities. Even black mourning clothes ceased to be worn because black wool fabric came from England. This economic boycott so hurt the British that eventually the Townshend taxes were rescinded, save for a small tax on tea. The Crown could not repeal all taxes without appearing to accept the possibility that the colonists were right in their stand of "no taxation without representation."

When the *Eleanor, Dartmouth,* and *Beaver* entered Boston Harbor, the Royal Governor of Massachusetts Bay Colony, Thomas Hutchinson, insisted that they be unloaded and their cargoes sold according to the provisions of the Tea Act. He owned one of the cargoes. The other owners and almost everyone else in Boston hoped that the vessels would simply head back out to sea. Hutchinson, unmoved, double-shotted the cannon at the British fort in the harbor and stationed two warships in the channel.

On December 16 the citizens of Boston held a mass meeting at the Old South Meeting House. While British military leaders focused on the great assembly where Adams and Quincy were haranguing the crowd, another, much smaller meeting was taking place in the back rooms of a printing shop. Availing themselves of a large bowl of potent fishhouse punch, Boston's Sons of Liberty transformed themselves into Mohawk Indians, complete with feathers, blankets, war paint, and tomahawks. John Adams noted later, however, "They were no ordinary Mohawks."

Early that Saturday evening, just as the meeting at Old South broke up, these "Mohawks" went on the warpath, leading the crowd to the bottom of Pearl Street, where the East India Company ships lay at Griffin's Wharf. With whoops and hollers, eighty or so "braves" clambered aboard the three vessels, broke open tea cases, and flung them into the sea. In less than three hours, they had destroyed all 342 chests of tea. The Redcoats never appeared; the British guns

Relive history aboard the Eleanor, Dartmouth, *and* Beaver *and celebrate one of Boston's pivotal moments at the Tea Party Ships and Museum.*

never fired; the ships were not damaged; and no one was hurt. The Tea Party was a resounding success.

The next morning tons of soggy East India Company tea washed ashore. It was the beginning of the end for England in America. Boston and its "Mohawks" had successfully defied the Crown in an act that electrified the colonies and made independence seem possible.

BOSTON TEA PARTY SHIPS
AND MUSEUM INFORMATION

HOURS: This site was undergoing renovations when this guide went to press; please call for hours and admission prices before you visit

PHONE: (617) 338-1773

WEB SITE: www.bostonteapartyship.com

PAUL REVERE'S HOUSE
19 North Square

Paul Revere's House is the only seventeenth-century wooden dwelling still standing in any major American city. Originally this was the site of the parsonage of the famous Increase Mather, autocratic minister of the first Old North Church and father of his eminent successor, diarist and witch-hunter the Reverend Cotton Mather. The house was about a hundred years old when Revere acquired it, and it was from here that he launched his famous ride to Lexington.

The Mather residence was one of forty-five houses destroyed in the Great Fire of November 18, 1676. Within a

Paul Revere's House is the only seventeenth-century wooden dwelling still standing in any major American city. COURTESY OF MOTT

year John Jeffs, a mariner, built another house on the site, which he sold in 1681 to merchant Robert Howard. The new house, typical of seventeenth-century Massachusetts architecture, was built in the English medieval style of the period, with a steep pitch roof; a front overhang, and at the attic level, a gable overhang, both with ornamental drops; small casement windows with diamond-shaped panes; and a simple floor plan that included a massive end chimney.

By contemporary standards the house was unusually spacious, having two large rooms in the front and two more in an ell that extended back toward the garden. The whole structure was framed in heavy carved timbers held together by ingenious joinery and wooden pegs.

Here Robert Howard and his successors dwelled one block from the sea, overlooking triangular North Square with its market, guardhouse, meetinghouse, and pump—a veritable beehive of industry and information and one of the town's most fashionable neighborhoods.

It was still a prime location in 1770, when Paul Revere purchased the Howard house for £213⅓ with a mortgage of £160 and moved in with his large family.

Revere, the son of a Huguenot, a Protestant refugee from France named Apollos Rivoire, was the talented possessor of a wide variety of skills and of industry enough to make good use of them. The proprietor of a Hancock's Wharf shop in which he fashioned objects of gold and silver, Revere was also a designer/engraver of copperplate; a manufacturer of false teeth; the owner of a bell foundry and copper works; the designer, engraver, and printer of the Commonwealth's paper money; a Son of Liberty and prominent rebel organizer; and an excellent horseman who rode as official courier of the Second Continental Congress. He also turned his hand to architecture and added a third story to the old house. In the age before specialization, he was Boston's preeminent generalist.

Today Revere is remembered for his midnight ride rather than for his bills and bells and bowls. The galloping rhythms and stirring language of Henry Wadsworth Longfellow's ballad, published in 1863, made Paul Revere one of the most celebrated heroes of the American Revolution. With the possible exception of "Twas the Night Before Christmas," "Paul Revere's Ride" may be the only poem of which every American can recite at least one couplet.

After the Revolution Revere settled down to a life of hard and rewarding work as one of the nation's first industrialists, developing his bell foundry and copper works, as well as a cannon foundry, into important Boston enterprises.

Revere sold his house in 1800, when he moved to more elegant quarters, but the three-story North Square building remained associated with his memory and was preserved through many years of neighborhood demolition and renewal.

The Paul Revere Memorial Association acquired the house in 1907 and, during the next two years, sheared off the third story and restored the building to its probable 1676 appearance. Today it is a showcase for some beautiful old furniture and china (not much of it is Revere's), two enormous fireplaces with brick ovens and antique utensils, portions of 1750 wallpaper depicting in block pattern the Church of Saint Mary-le-Bow in London, and an assortment of Revere's etchings and manuscript letters. Except for the Revere memorabilia, its most famous owner might have difficulty recognizing his residence, but John Jeffs, Robert Howard, and even Increase Mather would feel right at home.

PAUL REVERE'S HOUSE INFORMATION

HOURS: 9:30 a.m. to 5:15 p.m. daily, April 15 through October 31; 9:30 a.m. to 4:15 p.m. daily, November 1 through April 14 (except closed Monday, January through March); closed Thanksgiving, Christmas, and New Year's Day

ADMISSION: Adults, $3.00; seniors and students, $2.50; ages five to seventeen, $1.00

PHONE: (617) 523-2338

WEB SITE: www.paulreverehouse.org

WHEELCHAIR ACCESSIBILITY: Courtyard, first floor, and program area

SAINT STEPHEN'S CHURCH
Hanover Street, Facing the Prado

Saint Stephen's Church, originally the New North Congregational Church, is the only house of worship designed by Charles Bulfinch that is still standing in Boston. The church features a pilastered facade in what is described as a "bold and commanding style," surmounted by a clock tower, a belfry, and an Eastern dome. Bulfinch relieved the front elevation with a Palladian window, a lunette above, and his characteristic graceful blind-arch windows.

Bulfinch's church cost $26,570 to build. The cornerstone was laid on September 23, 1802, and the building dedicated on May 2, 1804. The following year the congregation purchased a bell for $800 from the foundry of Paul Revere. And in 1830 the church acquired an organ made by William Marcellus Goodrich, the leading organ maker in America.

The congregation already had a long history before it acquired the building. In 1714 seventeen successful Boston artisans had banded together to form a religious society that, they said, would provide spiritual sustenance to the city's

---

WHAT ONCE WAS . . .

In 1870, to accommodate the widening of Hanover Street, Saint Stephen's was moved back 16 feet and raised 6 inches on its foundation.

In 1964 Boston's Richard Cardinal Cushing authorized a complete restoration of Saint Stephen's, including restoring Bulfinch's cupola, which had been changed when the Catholic Church acquired the building in 1862, and lowering the building to its original foundation height. In the course of this project, workmen discovered the original side-entrance doors, bricked up, with hardware intact. Now Bulfinch's church once again looks much as he intended.

Saint Stephen's Church is the only Bulfinch-designed house of worship still standing in Boston.

"humble" citizens. "Unassisted by the more wealthy part of the community except by their prayers and good wishes," the artisans erected the New North Church building, a small wooden meetinghouse.

Under the Reverend John Webb, the society prospered. But in 1719, with the introduction of the Reverend Peter Thatcher as Webb's colleague, a bitter and messy division developed within the group. As a result a minority broke away to found the New Brick North Church. They topped their new house of worship with the city's first weathercock. According to local legend, the weathervane was barely installed on its perch when a gust of wind turned the cockerel's head in the direction of New North. A bystander, aware that the cock is a symbol of the Apostle Peter's denial and that Reverend Thatcher's first name was Peter, derisively crowed three times in the direction of New North. The New Brick was therefore also called "Revenge Church" and the "Cockerel Church." After the New Brick North Church was razed in 1871, the weathervane found a perch on the spire of First Church in Cambridge, Congregational, where it can be seen today.

In 1730 New North was enlarged. The congregation continued to grow and after the Revolution required a larger home. Down came the old wooden New North, and in its place rose a new brick New North (not to be confused with the New Brick North Church), using some of the old building's timbers.

Like many other congregations in the early part of the nineteenth century, New North's adopted Unitarianism. In

1814, the church was renamed the Second Unitarian Church. As early as the 1820s, however, the North End was changing, and by the 1850s the area had become solidly Irish Catholic. In 1862 Father John J. Williams, administrator at the time and later Archbishop of Boston, purchased the church and dedicated it to Saint Stephen, the first Christian martyr. By 1900, however, the Irish of the North End were replaced by the Italians, whose descendants continue to worship here.

SAINT STEPHEN'S CHURCH INFORMATION

HOURS: Open daily at 7:30 a.m.; Mass is held Sunday at 11:00 a.m., Tuesday through Friday at 7:30 a.m., and Saturday at 4:30 p.m.

ADMISSION: Free

PHONE: (617) 523-1230

WHEELCHAIR ACCESSIBILITY: No

PAUL REVERE MALL
Hanover Street, Next to the Old North Church

Paul Revere Mall, the small park linking Christ Church ("Old North") and Saint Stephen's Church, is dominated by Cyrus Dallin's equestrian statue of that celebrated midnight rider, Paul Revere. Thirteen bronze plaques set in the Prado walls recount the role that the North End and its people played in the history of Boston from 1630 to 1918.

The North End's most famous resident by far, Paul Revere rode from Boston to Lexington on April 18, 1775, to bring the latest intelligence about the British to John Hancock and

Paul Revere rides tall with the steeple of the Old North Church in the back-ground. COURTESY OF THE GREATER BOSTON CONVENTION & VISITORS BUREAU

Samuel Adams. General Thomas Gage and his troops were preparing to march out and capture the colonial militia's contraband muskets, gunpowder, and cannons stored in Concord. No one knew, however, when the British would march or the route they would take.

On the evening of April 18, 1775, Redcoats began to gather on Boston Common. It soon became apparent that their destination was Lexington and Concord. At about eleven o'clock that evening, the light of two lanterns shone from the steeple of Christ Church. This was Revere's prearranged signal to the patriots in Charlestown that the British would be advancing from Boston by a water route to the Charlestown shore, and then to Concord. Revere wrapped himself in a heavy cloak, slipped down to the waterfront, and "with muffled oar, silently rowed to the Charlestown shore," safely passing by the illuminated man-o'-war *Somerset*. Just as the moonlight revealed British transport barges rounding the point, Revere docked quietly and mounted Deacon Larkin's sturdy horse.

The rest is history, or poetry. Revere rode off through Cambridge to Medford, and from Medford to Lexington, calling, "The British are coming." He thundered past sleeping farms, dismounting and pounding on doors at every village common or knot of country homes. Behind him he left bells ringing and men shouting and dogs barking. Minutemen poured out of their homes to form ranks against the enemy. Other horsemen saddled up and rode off to spread the word. By the time Revere reached Lexington, the whole countryside was up in arms.

Before dawn Revere was captured between Lexington and Concord by an advance party of British cavalry. They detained him until their troops had marched past on the way to Lexington Common. His captors had no way of knowing that the Yankee horseman they held had ruined their plans.

For before the sun went down that day, the militia of Massachusetts gave His Majesty's troops a terrible beating. It was the first day of the Revolutionary War.

OLD NORTH CHURCH
193 Salem Street

The building we know today as Old North Church, also called Christ Church, was erected in 1723; it is the oldest house of worship still standing in Boston. The second Episcopal church in Boston—the first is King's Chapel—it was designed by the Boston print-seller William Price in the manner of Sir Christopher Wren's London churches. The original brick tower was surmounted by one of the architectural wonders of Old Boston, a magnificent spire soaring 191 feet above the street.

Old North Church, once a bastion of Loyalist support for the British Empire, may be the best-known landmark of the Revolutionary era. Thanks to Henry Wadsworth Longfellow's poem "Paul Revere's Ride," every schoolchild in America learns that Revere's ride was triggered by a lantern signal: "One if by land, and two if by sea."

The church sexton, Robert Newman, was a friend of Revere and shone the lanterns on the night of April 18, 1775, thus alerting the Charlestown rebels of the British intention to cross over to their shore. Revere himself, as he rowed out on the flood tide, must have seen the double

A FINAL RESTING PLACE

The British leader of the Lexington-Concord expedition, Major John Pitcairn, died heroically at Bunker Hill and is said to be buried in a vault below the Old North Church.

HAPPY BICENTENNIAL

On April 18, 1975, President Gerald Ford inaugurated the nation's bicentennial year at the Old North Church.

light shining out from Christ Church. Before he even touched shore, the secret English invasion was common knowledge, the march on Concord revealed. (One of the lanterns spied by Paul Revere is on display at the Concord Museum.)

When British general Thomas Gage, who attended services at Christ Church (pew 62), chose the steeple as a vantage point from which to observe the burning of Charlestown and the British disaster at Bunker Hill, he probably did not know of the church's role in warning the patriots.

The historic steeple of Longfellow's poem—the gift of a group of merchants from British Honduras who in return received the use of a handsome box pew—came crashing down in the Great Gale of 1804. The steeple fell on an old tenement house, which was destroyed, but fortunately no one was injured. Charles Bulfinch, carefully preserving its "symmetry and proportions," provided a new design with a steeple that was 16 feet shorter. The Bulfinch steeple fell victim to a hurricane in 1954. The present steeple, a reproduction of the first, is capped with Shem Drowne's original 1740 weathervane, a banner with a ball and star above.

In 1744 Dr. Timothy Cutler, the spiritual leader of the congregation of wealthy and influential families, most of whom were connected with the Royal government of the province, sailed to Britain to obtain the chief ornament of the church: a marvelous chime of eight bells inscribed with such sentiments as "We are the first ring of bells cast for the British Empire in North America," "Since generosity has

Old North Church is the oldest house of worship still standing in Boston and is the site of the famous lantern hanging the night of Paul Revere's ride. © 2005

opened our mouths, our tongues shall ring aloud its praise," and, of course, "God preserve the Church of England." The carillon—young Paul Revere was one of the early bell ringers—still rings out with extraordinary beauty on Sundays after 11:00 a.m. service, on the Fourth of July, and for every major historical occasion, including presidential inaugurations.

Many of the church's interior fittings were donated by philanthropic Englishmen interested in propagating the doctrines of the Church of England in Puritan Boston. King George II himself donated the silver communion service. Captain Thomas Gruchy, commander of the privateer *Queen of Hungary,* presented the four trumpeting angels that grace the choir loft, booty from a French vessel.

After more than two centuries, Old North Church is still an active Episcopal congregation, with services on Sunday mornings. Brass plates on the pews bear names of Revolutionary-era families, many of whose descendants still worship here, including those of Paul Revere (pew 54). The bust of George Washington at the front of the church is a fine likeness of the president, according to the Marquis de Lafayette.

Incidentally, this is not Boston's first Old North Church. The old Old North Church, built in 1650 in North Square, was destroyed by fire in 1676, was rebuilt, and stood for another hundred years before the British tore it down for firewood.

COPP'S HILL

Hull and Snowhill Streets

Copp's Hill Burial Ground in the North End, Boston's second-oldest cemetery, comprises three or four graveyards of different periods. The oldest, in the northeasterly section bounded by Charter and Snowhill Streets, dates from 1660.

The area near Snowhill Street was reserved for slave burials, although the tall black monument near the Snowhill Street fence is a memorial to Prince Hall, a freed slave and leader of Boston's free black community. He helped sponsor Boston's first school for black children and founded the African Grand Lodge of Massachusetts, the world's first black Masonic lodge. About 1,000 free blacks are also buried here.

Most were residents of New Guinea, a pre-Revolutionary community at the foot of the hill.

Although many of Copp's Hill's old stones are gone, appropriated years ago by North Enders for chimneys and doorsteps, the heraldic markers set in the west wall remain, and the cemetery is filled with wonderful epitaphs and tombstones with quaint inscriptions.

Here lie the mortal remains of Messrs. Milk and Beer and of Mistresses Brown, Scarlet, and White. Close by are the stones of Samuel Mower and Theodocia Hay. The illustrious Mathers, for several generations the theological dictators of Boston, are interred in their family tomb. And Edmund Hartt, builder of the USS *Constitution,* rests within cannon shot of his creation. Robert Newman, the sexton who signaled Paul Revere with two lanterns hung in the steeple of Old North Church, is buried here, too.

In the early 1600s a fort occupied the hill, which has also been known as Snow Hill, Mill Field, and Windmill Hill. Boston's first windmill was acquired in August 1632 from Cambridge, where it failed to grind except with a westerly wind. Atop this hill it successfully caught ocean breezes to grind corn for the city's early settlers.

The Old North Burying Ground was set aside in 1659 for North End residents. It is now named for William Copp, a shoemaker who settled in the North End after emigrating from Stratford-upon-Avon, England. He owned the land before selling it to the town for a cemetery and is buried here, too.

By the time of the Revolution, several shipyards and wharves had been established at the base of Copp's Hill. Its crest commanded an excellent view of Boston and, across the Charles River, of Charlestown. Here in June 1775 the British set up a battery that bombarded Charlestown during the Battle of Bunker Hill and set that town ablaze. Generals John

Many gravestones at Copp's Hill bear the pockmarks of musket balls; some were even used for target practice by the British soldiers.

Burgoyne and Henry Clinton used Copp's Hill as a command post during the battle and were witness to the doubly grisly sight of an entire town burning to the ground and, just beyond, an army of British regulars falling dead or wounded.

Many gravestones bear the pockmarks of musket balls. The chipped stone of Captain Daniel Malcolm, "A True Son of Liberty . . . an enemy to Oppression," bears testimony to the pleasure of British troops in using it for target practice.

Like Beacon Hill, Copp's Hill was once a good deal higher. It presented an almost sheer cliff to the water side, sloping gradually back toward the town as a three-acre field. The crest of the hill was removed in 1807 for use as a mill-pond landfill, where North Station now sits, and the site of both the windmill and the British battery disappeared into the mud. For more than a decade, the hill was diminished for fill. Yet Copp's Hill endures, an irreducible element of Old Boston.

COPP'S HILL INFORMATION

HOURS: 9:00 a.m. to 5:00 p.m. daily

ADMISSION: Free

PHONE: (617) 635-7389

WHEELCHAIR ACCESSIBILITY: No

USS CONSTITUTION
Charlestown Navy Yard

The USS *Constitution,* launched on October 12, 1797, is the oldest commissioned warship afloat in the world.

After the American Revolution, the American Navy was disbanded, and for more than a decade no warships sailed under the Stars and Stripes. By 1793, however, the Barbary pirates of North Africa were preying on U.S. merchant vessels, demanding tribute and ransom, so in March 1794 President George Washington approved an act to build six ships for the defense of the nation.

During the summer of 1795, Edmund Hartt laid the white oak keel of a frigate, built to carry forty-four guns, at his North End shipyard. Although peace was made that fall with the ruler of Algiers, work continued for two years on the *Constitution.* Its timbers were white oak from New Jersey, New Hampshire, and Massachusetts; live oak from Saint

Simons Island of Georgia; and yellow pine from Georgia and the Carolinas. Its white pine masts came from Maine; its copper bolts and spikes, from Paul Revere's foundry.

Measuring 204 feet from stem to stern and 44 feet broad, the vessel carried fifty-four guns and 450 men. It displaced 2,200 tons and could carry provisions for a crew of 475. Its mainmast towered 189 feet into the sky, and its sails, comprising nearly an acre of canvas, were constructed at the Old Granary, the only building large enough to accommodate the work. The Skillings brothers carved the original figurehead of Hercules presenting a scroll, symbolic of the Constitution of the United States.

By July 1798 the United States had become involved in an undeclared war with France, and the *Constitution* was sent on patrol in the West Indies until a settlement could be reached.

In 1803 the *Constitution* was the flagship of a squadron sent to attack the persistent corsairs of Tripoli. Under Commodore Edward Preble the frigate pounded Tripoli into submission. In the end the governor of Tripoli came aboard to initial a draft of the peace treaty.

The United States wished to remain neutral in the war that had broken out between France and Great Britain in 1803, but after years of increasing British harassment of American shipping, Congress declared war on Britain in June 1812. A British journalist voiced his country's scornful attitude toward the action, writing that "fir-built" American frigates "manned by a handful of bastards and outlaws" were no match for the British Navy.

Nevertheless, on August 19, 1812, under Captain Isaac Hull the *Constitution* achieved what historians cite as "probably the most brilliant American victory of the war." She engaged the forty-nine-gun British frigate *Guerriere* off Nova Scotia and within an hour reduced the ship to a hulk. Having watched enemy cannonballs bounce off the *Constitution's*

The USS Constitution *was known as "Old Ironsides" because enemy cannonballs bounced off her sturdy hull.* COURTESY OF THE GREATER BOSTON CONVENTION & VISITORS BUREAU sturdy hull, crewmen celebrated their ship's first naval victory, dubbing her "Old Ironsides."

Under a new captain, William Bainbridge, the *Constitution* continued its record of outstanding service. On December 29, 1812, off the coast of Brazil, after a spirited and terrible exchange of broadsides, the forty-seven-gun frigate *Java* was demasted and her commander fatally wounded. A lieutenant ordered the colors struck, and the British frigate was blown up.

Two years later, under Captain Charles Stewart, the intrepid *Constitution* engaged the British warships *Cyane* and *Levant* off the coast of Portugal. With skillful maneuvering and deadly cannon fire, "Old Ironsides" soon made a wreck of the *Cyane*. The *Levant* fought on and nearly escaped but returned to battle and fell prey to the larger American vessel.

Thus ended the illustrious fighting career of the USS *Constitution*. She was in forty battles and was never beaten and never boarded.

The warship retired to Boston, where it remained until 1821, when it cruised the Mediterranean. It returned in 1828 to rumors that the U.S. Navy had decided to scrap it, and in 1830, condemned as unseaworthy, the *Constitution* was ordered destroyed. A student at Harvard, Oliver Wendell Holmes, responded with a poem of protest. His verse provoked such an outcry that Congress appropriated funds to restore the frigate.

By 1897, one hundred years after her maiden voyage, the ship was rotting away. In his campaign to save the vessel, John F. Fitzgerald, maternal grandfather of President John F. Kennedy, spoke before Congress and presented a resolution to preserve the frigate as a memorial. Congress authorized repairs so minimal, however, that in 1905 the historic ship was again headed for destruction, this time as a training target for the fleet.

Americans protested, and Congress appropriated $100,000 for additional repairs. For the next twenty years, the ship remained at her pier in Boston as a museum but continued to decay. Congress had little enthusiasm for preserving the *Constitution,* enacting a bill in 1925 that authorized reconstruction but provided no funds for the work. After a public fund-raising campaign—even schoolchildren answered the call by donating their pennies—the collected sum still fell short of what was needed. Finally Congress appropriated money to complete the work.

Totally overhauled, the *Constitution* departed Boston on July 2, 1931, on one of the longest voyages of her career—more than three years and ninety-one ports—greeted everywhere by admiring crowds. Afterward she returned to her home port, where for more than fifty years she has served as flagship for Commandants of the First Naval District.

Now the *Constitution* is berthed at the Charlestown Navy Yard, next to her newer neighbor, the World War II destroyer USS *Cassin Young.* Once a year "Old Ironsides" sails into Boston Harbor for a turnaround cruise, honored with a cortege of streaming fireboats.

USS CONSTITUTION INFORMATION

HOURS: 10:00 a.m. to 5:50 p.m. Tuesday through Sunday, April 1 through October 31; 10:00 a.m. to 3:50 p.m. Thursday through Sunday, November 1 through March 31. Tours begin every thirty minutes, with the last tour beginning at 3:30 p.m.

ADMISSION: Free

PHONE: (617) 242-5670 or 242-5671

WEB SITE: www.ussconstitution.navy.mil

WHEELCHAIR ACCESSIBILITY: Yes

BUNKER HILL

Charlestown

Both the British and the colonists made so many mistakes during the Battle of Bunker Hill that some historians call it the "Battle of Blunders."

Not only did the colonists fortify the wrong hill, Breed's Hill, but they also dug themselves into a trap with a narrow escape. The British, on the other hand, so disdained their ragtag opponents that they ignored good military strategy. Instead of closing the trap, they routed the citizen soldiers, and the majority escaped.

Providing protective cover for the retreating colonials, however, cost the life of the much-loved Dr. Joseph Warren. The physician had served as president of the provincial congress and chairman of the Massachusetts Committee on Safety, an interim government the colony established after the Royal Governor departed.

Fought on June 17, 1775, the first major battle of the Revolutionary War was also the bloodiest. More than 1,400 men, mostly British soldiers, died in an hour and a half. British general Thomas Gage noted, "The rebels are not the despicable rabble too many have supposed."

Still, the colonials lost the battle. But it was not for lack of courage. One of at least six black soldiers, twenty-eight-year-old Salem Poor, who went on to fight with George Washington at Valley Forge, was honored with a 1976 bicentennial postage stamp as a "gallant soldier." Notwithstanding the patriots' defeat, Charlestown observes the battle's anniversary with pomp and parades every June 17.

As for the famous Quincy granite monument, it almost didn't get off the ground. On June 17, 1825, the fiftieth anniversary of the battle, the cornerstone was laid with great fanfare. Trowel in hand, the Marquis de Lafayette, the nation's guest, spread the mortar. Two hundred veterans of the Revolutionary War, including forty who had fought in the celebrated engagement, looked on. Daniel Webster, the rousing orator, proclaimed, "The consequences of the Battle of Bunker Hill are greater than those of any ordinary conflict."

But the venture, which had begun so optimistically, experienced setbacks. The foundation proved inadequate; the cornerstone was quietly relocated. Construction started anew, but the tower was barely 40 feet high when money ran out. The architect and builder, Solomon Willard, donated his services as a "patriotic duty." The project, however, was abandoned, $23,000 in debt.

Another attempt to complete the monument began in 1834. About 45 feet were added before work was again halted for lack of funds. The memorial, undertaken with high hopes, became a public joke. Neighbors proposed to tear down the eyesore. It probably would have been razed, had not a feisty lady from Maine stepped in.

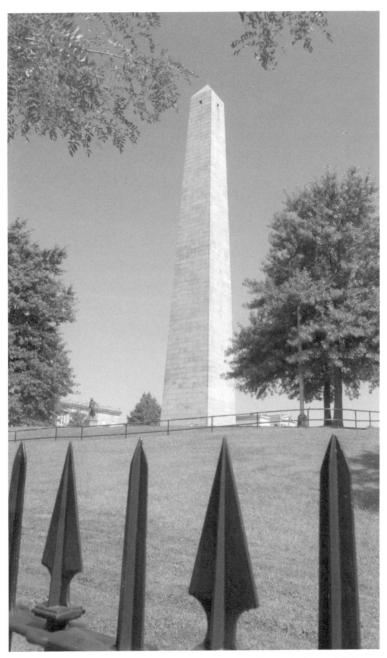

The monument on Bunker Hill was truly a group effort and almost didn't happen at all. COURTESY OF THE GREATER BOSTON CONVENTION & VISITORS BUREAU

Up, Up . . .

Visitors may climb 294 steps of the monument at Bunker Hill for a view of Boston. Be warned, however, there is no elevator.

When she arrived in Boston in 1828, Sarah Josepha Hale, the fervently patriotic daughter of a Revolutionary War officer, was a recent widow and the sole support of five young children. Her imagination and emotions were immediately engaged by the drive to erect the monument, and she began writing editorials favorable to the endeavor in the *Ladies' Magazine,* precursor of *Godey's Lady's Book.* Then she took the unprecedented step of conducting a public fund-raising drive.

At first members of the Monument Association, all men, refused to cooperate with Widow Hale. Finally they accepted her help on condition that the "efforts of the ladies will not degrade the character of men."

With the publication of her patriotic poem "The Last of the Band," Hale raised the first $3,000 of the $100,000 required to complete the monument. Then she rented Quincy Hall, the largest exposition space in Boston, for a fair.

Throughout the summer of 1840, New England women and women from as far away as Ohio and the Carolinas busily sewed, embroidered, prepared straw work, beaded, quilted, did waxwork, put up jellies and pickles, and produced whatever their hands could contrive. When the fair opened on September 8, more than 4,000 people attended. Seven days later it closed, and after all expenses had been paid out, the women's earnings exceeded $30,000. In the Monument Association report, the men acknowledged that the sum was "beyond expectations."

The effort was now supported by newspapers throughout New England; donations poured in. When the fund was

$20,000 short, Amos Lawrence, a Boston merchant, pledged $10,000 if someone else would match it. Judah Touro, the orphaned son of the rabbi of a synagogue in Newport, Rhode Island, had as a youth been taken in by an aunt in Boston. Now a successful entrepreneur, he donated the money to top off the 221-foot, 294-step granite obelisk. He had wished to remain anonymous, but on June 17, 1843, at the monument's dedication ceremonies, attended by President John Tyler and his entire cabinet, the two benefactors were acknowledged.

> *Amos and Judah, venerated names;*
> *Patriarch and Prophet press their equal claim.*
> *Christian and Jew, they carry out one plan,*
> *For though of different faith,*
> *Each is in heart a man.*

At last the first monument built through public donation was completed. Sarah Josepha Hale is credited with organizing the first women's auxiliary, a model for women's clubs that helped men achieve their goals. Bunker Hill Monument is generally considered the first publicized tourist attraction and the first historic site in America to be restored.

BUNKER HILL INFORMATION

HOURS: 9:00 a.m. to 4:30 p.m. daily; lodge with displays open until 5:00 p.m.; closed Thanksgiving, Christmas, and New Year's Day

ADMISSION: Free

PHONE: (617) 242-5641

WHEELCHAIR ACCESSIBILITY: Restrooms and lodge

INDEX